BENTWORTH

The Making of a Hampshire Village

Georgia Smith

Published by

Bentworth Parochial Church Council
The Rectory, Bentworth, Alton, Hampshire.

© Georgia Smith 1988

ISBN 0 9513653 0 4

Printed by
Rodek Printing, Unit 6 Forge Works,
Mill Lane, Alton, Hampshire.

Contents

Illustrations	ii
Acknowledgements	iii
Introduction	1
The Royal Charters	5
The Medieval Village	7
After the Black Death	13
The Village During the Reformation	18
New Houses in the Stuart Village	24
New Land Owners	35
Thomas Coulthard	41
The Beginnings of the Modern Village	49
Select Bibliography	58
Index	59

Illustrations

Bentworth Church, c.1840.	3
The Charter of Henry II to Archbishop Hugh of Rouen, 1155. (Archives Departementales, Departement de la Seine-Maritime, Rouen)	4
Hall Farm c.1890.	9
The medieval parish of Bentworth	10
The Windsor, Bentworth family connection.	14
Henry, 5th Baron Windsor. (Private Collection. Photograph, Courtauld Institute of Art)	22
George Wither, by John Payne	27
Detail from the Map of Wivelrod Farm, 1742.	38
Swains Farmhouse	43
Farmhouses in the centre of the village	44
The Magewick, Battin, Coulthard family.	47
The centre of the village, from the Tithe Map of 1840. (Hampshire Record Office)	53
The Village Green c.1905.	54

Acknowledgement

I would like to thank all those members of the Staff of the Hampshire Record Office who over many years have given me so much assistance and encouragement in the search for the history of Bentworth.

Introduction

Bentworth lies hidden in the wooded, closely folded hills which form the south eastern end of the Hampshire Downs. The area, about fifteen miles long and five miles wide, is dotted with a chain of villages from Herriard to Froxfield whose histories are diverse, and have yet to be studied on a regional basis. They are sited on the Upper Chalk where it is extensively covered with Clay-with-Flints and forms the geological boundary between the great spread of the chalk downland to the west and the Weald to the east.

Almost all the land of the parish is within the five hundred and seven hundred feet contours, and there is no surface water. To meet the need for water, every farm and small settlement had at least one pond, and often several, most of which have now been filled in, but still account for bends in the road, and areas of scrub on the verge. In addition there was a village well in a combe of the downs to the east of the village centre. Part of the eastern boundary of the parish, until recently marked by the line of the Basingstoke – Alton road, follows a dry valley which terminates at Willhall, a Domesday farm sited at the source of the river Wey inside the Alton border. Another dry valley, from Wield on the west to Lasham on the east, was part of a medieval road from Winchester which entered the parish at Ashley, and followed a line of gravel to Rother Hatch where it passed a cattle gate on the old road through the village between Alton and Basingstoke. Curving round the ridge of high ground at the centre of the village, there is on the east and south a third valley which provided the most suitable land for the open fields.

Settled by the Saxons, the documented history of Bentworth began in the early decades of the 12th century with a grant of the manor of Bentworth by Henry I to the Archbishop of Rouen. Manorial records have survived in various broken series, and there is a wealth of other sources of information. The village is also lucky in its surviving buildings which are part of the visual expression of its history. The church and the medieval hall house, now Hall Farm, arouse the curiosity and interest of residents and strangers, and the later styles of vernacular architecture, the timber frames of the 16th and 17th centuries, the flint and brick of the 18th and 19th centuries are attractive markers in its later development.

An annotated typescript of this study will be deposited in the Hampshire Record Office where most of the sources of information, either in the original form or as copies, are to be found. I hope from this starting point others will be encouraged to make more in-depth studies of the many aspects of Bentworth's long history.

Bentworth Church c.1840.

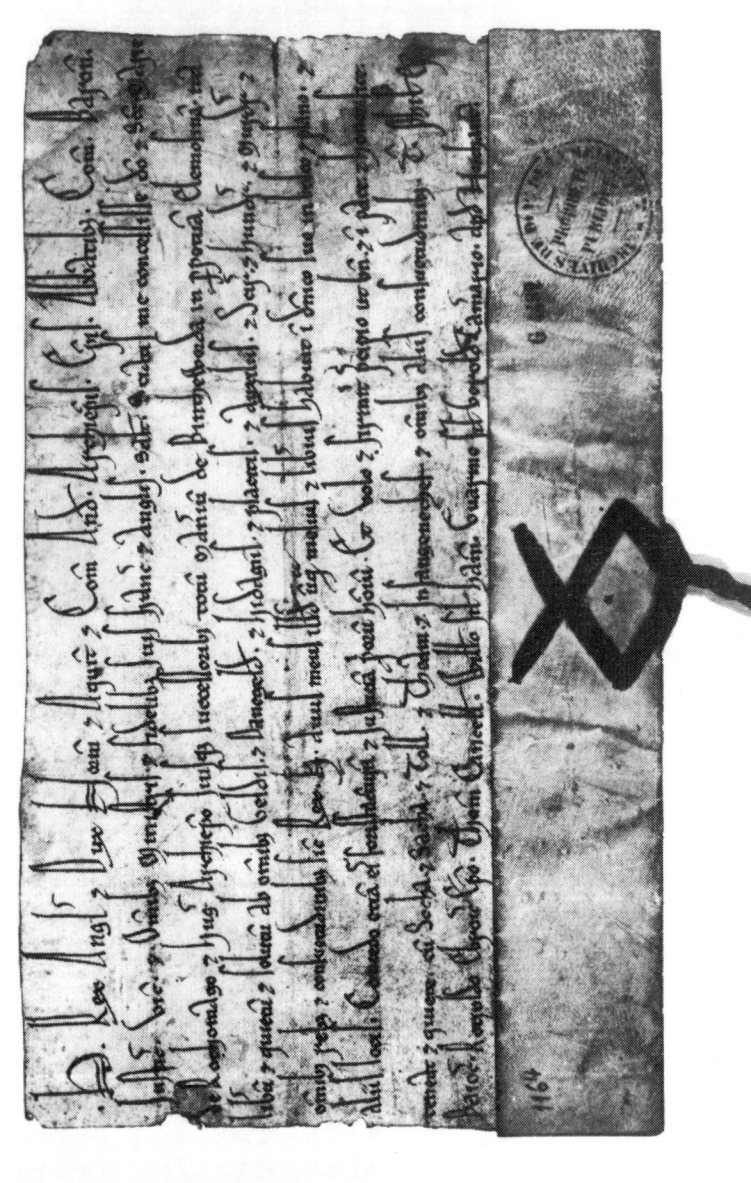

The Charter of Henry II to Archbishop Hugh in 1155 renewing the previous grant by Henry I.

ROYAL CHARTERS

THE MANOR of BENTWORTH and THE CHURCH

'Know that I have given to God and to St. Mary, and Geoffrey Archbishop of Rouen and his successors, for the soul of my father King William and my mother Queen Matilda, and of King William my brother, and for my soul and health and of Queen Matilda my wife and our children, the manor which is called Bynteworda with the berewica called Bercheham.'

With those words Henry I, King of England, Duke of Normandy, and son of William the Conqueror, gave the manor of Bentworth and the berewick, or outlying farm, at Burkham to his friend and spiritual mentor Geoffrey, Archbishop of Rouen, the primate of Normandy. The court was at Windsor and the date February 2nd, the Feast of the Purification of the Virgin, but as in most early documents, the year was not stated. The presence of certain witnesses points to it having been between the years 1111 and 1116. As the Domesday commissioners of 1086 did not record the village in their survey, perhaps because its isolated settlements were included in the summarised account of the king's land in Odiham Hundred, the charter is the earliest known document in the history of Bentworth.

About fifty years later, in 1165, Henry II – Henry Plantagenet – granted the church of Bentworth to Rotrou, the then Archbishop of Rouen. The charter makes no reference to the dedication. If the church was of Saxon origin like the settlements, as the place names suggest that they were, its first dedication was probably different, and changed to St. Mary to accord with the terms of the king's gift, and the dedication of the cathedral at Rouen.

    Nikolaus Pevsner in his survey of Hampshire in The Buildings of England series, remarked on the number of churches where the architectural style belongs to the transitional period between Norman and Early English, about 1180 – 1220. The arcades of the nave in the church at Bentworth are examples of just such work. The sturdy round pillars, with multi-scalloped capitals and square abaci, which are in the Norman tradition, carry pointed – instead of rounded arches – which are an early expression of the new style.

    Work on enlarging the chancel was undertaken a little later, and is truly Early English in style. The east window consists of three pointed lights, stepped and separately set into the walling. The group is enclosed by a moulded pointed arch with dog tooth ornament, and a hood mould with carved label stops. The shafts of the arch have moulded capitals, but the bases are hidden by the nineteenth century Italian reredos. The trefoil piscina has moulding and dog tooth decoration, again of the Early English period. There are two lancet lights with widely splayed jambs in the north wall, and two wider lancets in the south wall with a priest's door between them. The internal arch of the doorway has a simple chamfer, but externally it is finely moulded and finished with small carved label stops.

    In the late twelfth century when the nave of the church was being built, the Archbishops of Rouen were still in close touch with the Kings of England. Rotrou, who had worked for a reconciliation between Henry II and Thomas Becket (murdered in 1170), was with the king in Winchester in 1172. In 1189 Richard I reaffirmed the rights of the Archbishops, and two years later sent Archbishop Walter de Coutances to England specifically to look after the King's interests, threatened by his brother John. But after 1204 when King John lost Normandy, there was probably little or no contact with the Archbishops until Odon Rigaud came to Westminster to do fealty to Henry III in 1248. He journeyed on to Bentworth in all the splendour of a prelate of the period – to consecrate the rebuilt church? Or did he give orders for the work on the chancel to be done? The answer may lie in the archives in Rouen.

The Medieval Village

The names of the four settlements of Bentworth, Burkham, Wivelrod, and Ashley are all of Saxon origin, which suggests that they existed for sometime before the Conquest; but it is only early in the thirteenth century that a dimly perceived village, consisting of these settlements, begins to emerge from the records.

In 1223 Ralph de Aule held the free tenement of the Hall, or La Aule, as the Norman clerks called it. It was not the house at Hall Farm which stands today, (that was not built for another hundred years), but on the same site, or very near it. It was a good position, an area of level ground on a long downland ridge capped by clay with flints, and sheltered by oak and beech woods, the land falling away to the east and west. Close by would have been at least one of the many ponds which sustained the scattered settlements, and possibly a well. Behind the house, following the line of Tinkers Lane towards Wivelrod, lay South Field, one of the open fields. In front, bounded by Mucklands Lane and the woodland to west and north, lay West Field. At the north end of the ridge a large corner field was cleared between Drury Lane and Haley Lane to be known as Mill Field, and by the later medieval period, there was a fourth field called Ridge Field alongside Wadgetts Lane.

In 1259 William le Clerk and his wife Cicely, who had land at Wivelrod, leased it to Ralph de la Sale for an annual rent of one penny and one quarter of wheat and one of barley, delivered each Michaelmas for the rest of their lives. Before the end of the century Gilbert of Ashley was in possession of land described as bounded on one side by the highway from Winchester to Lasham, presumably a reference to the old track from Ashley along the valley marked now by Powells Farm to Haley Lane, and onwards to Lasham by way of Pedlars Lane.

Among those who witnessed the Ashley deed was Augustine of Burkham, and the name, perhaps borne by his son, appears in several more documents over the next forty years, in particular the tax return known as the Lay Subsidy of 1327. The tax collector identified eleven men and one woman as the wealthier inhabitants of the village. Together they paid 42s. 11d. in sums varying from 1s. 4d. to 3s. 2d. except for Matilda of Bentworth who paid 19s. much the largest amount for many miles around.

Matilda was the widow of William de Aule, at one time Constable of Farnham Castle, who in addition to his land in Bentworth, had a hundred acres in Basingstoke, more land at Chineham, Nately, and Tunworth, and a small farm at Bramley, which became known as Little Bentworth. It seems very likely that William started to build the present house at Hall Farm, and the work was continued after his death by Matilda, because in 1333 or soon after, she was granted the right to a private chapel, which is still standing at the south west corner of the house. Built of flint and stone, the thick outer walls of the house are largely unaltered, and follow the plan of a typical open hall house of the period. The entrance porch with outer and inner doorways of moulded stone led into a through-passage with the hall on the right open to the roof. This was the centre of the everyday life of the household, and the place where the manor courts were held. At the south end of the hall there was a two-storied wing containing the solar for the private use of the family. It is assumed that the north wing provided other domestic quarters and a service area, but the only visible medieval features are three narrow window openings, two in the north wall, one in the east gable.

The feudal link between Bentworth and Rouen which existed for two hundred years came to an end on the orders of Edward III in the opening phase of the Hundred Years War in 1336, perhaps while Matilda was still alive. The manor was promised to Richard of Bentworth, Matilda's surviving son and a cleric at the royal court, who was frequently abroad on diplomatic missions. However five months later it is recorded that William Melton, Archbishop of York, and the King's former Treasurer, was guilty of having taken possession without licence. Melton had obtained the manor of Kingsclere from the Canons of Rouen Cathedral and it seems he could not resist annexing the Archbishop's manor of Bentworth only twenty miles

Hall Farm c.1890. The former Chapel is on the right.

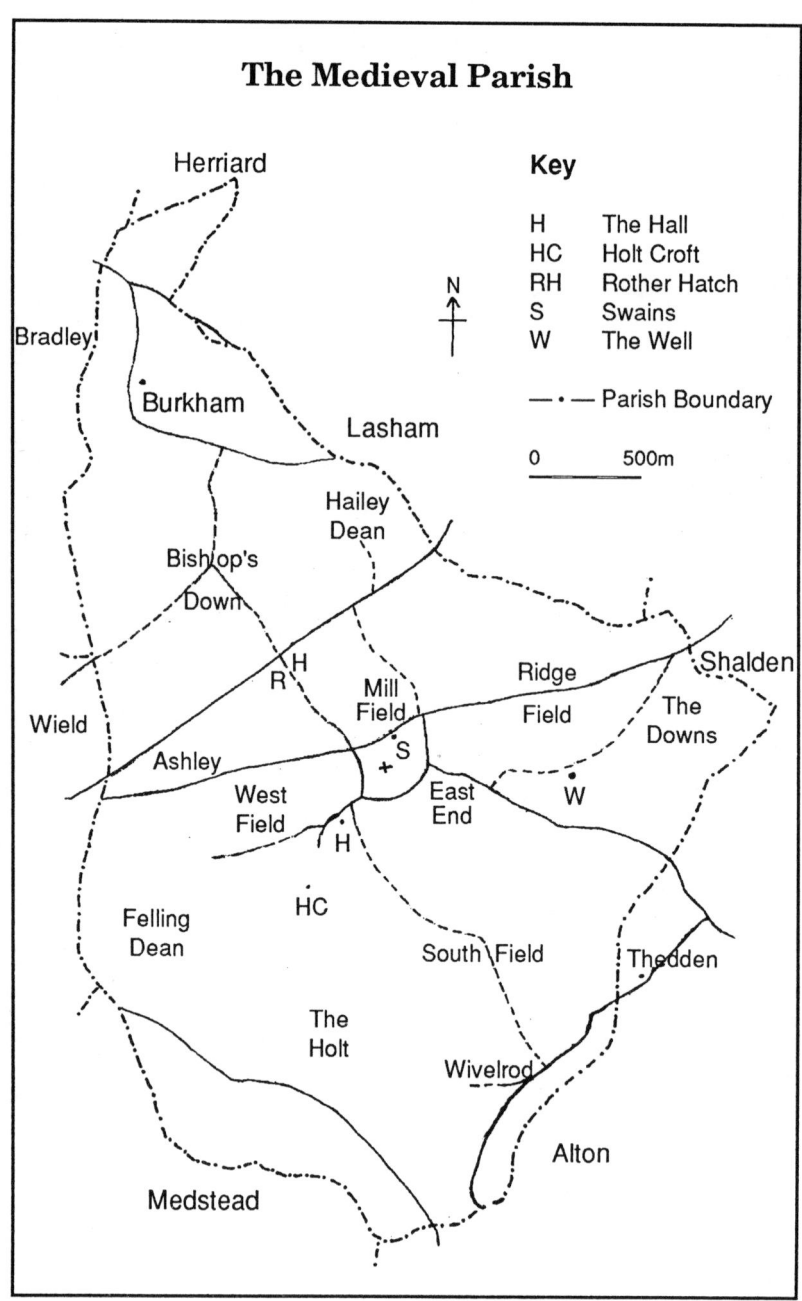

away. Together they made a better economic unit and he was an accomplished financier, to whom the Crown was indebted monetarily, morally and even militarily, because for years he had fought off the marauding Scots on the northern border. So whatever the King's displeasure at this cool regard for the royal prerogative, Melton obtained a grant of the manor, and Bentworth remained in his hands. On his death in 1340 the manor passed to his nephew, and subsequently to his descendants until 1510. Richard, who also lived only another four years, became Keeper of the Privy Seal, the King's Chancellor, and Bishop of London. Robbed of becoming overlord of his native village, he bought some seventy acres of land on the road to Burkham, which became known as Bishop's Down.

The names of men who were listed with Matilda in the Lay Subsidy of 1327, and were contemporary with men known to be alive in 1341, appear in the earliest known rent list of the manor of Bentworth Hall, that is the old tenement of the Hall, held more than a century before by Ralph de Aule, and more recently by William de Aule, otherwise William of Bentworth, Matilda's dead husband. The heading and date at the top of the parchment roll have been worn away, but it is possible to deduce that the list was drawn up a year or two after 1341.

Thirty three tenants were listed in the rental, including three blacksmiths, a weaver, tailor, and chapman. Unfortunately the miller was not identified. At least three families lived at Ashley; and also described then as living in the hamlet of Ashley was Isabel, widow of Henry atte Holte, the Saxon word for wood. She paid rent for a holding known as Holt Croft, now the site of the cricket field, which at that time was a clearing in the woods surrounding the village. Another five tenants and three cottagers lived at Wivelrod, and their neighbour Walter of Thedden had land on both sides of the parish boundary, as the farm still does today. John atte Slade, one of the men who paid the Lay Subsidy, took his name from the valley below Childer Hill, but was also a tenant of land with a grazing right at Ashley. A family named Battisford who stemmed from John Battisford, a King's Justice of Assize and a contemporary of Gilbert of Ashley, had several holdings. Part was still in family hands, an area of woodland was let to one of the blacksmiths, and part was let to Nicholas le Devenysh, a prominent Winchester family of merchants, originally from Exeter, who were tenants for three generations.

Grazing rights, particularly for cattle, may have been the reason also for the presence in the rental of three other outsiders, Henry of Merewelle, Roger of Northampton, and Walter of Tytherley; each paid the relatively high rent of 5s. 11d. per half year. The Saxon place name Rother Hatch, meaning a cattle gate, for a site near the present day entrance to Powells Farm in Burkham Lane, is a further indication that cattle raising was the traditional farming pattern for this land to the north of the village. Rent for the original 'berewick', a term often used of dairy farms, at Burkham was by this time paid "by right of his wife Alice", by John Cachefreynsh of Preston Candover, another man with property in Winchester. Altogether it seems that at least eight tenants on the list of thirty-three had interests well beyond the boundaries of the village. Perhaps these tenancies derived originally from the close association of the early Archbishops of Rouen with the English court sojourning at Winchester, and continued to be of value as grazing rights to merchants in Winchester.

After the Black Death

A rental of the 1340s is a precious survival, even though it provides only a tantalisingly limited glimpse of the old village. Within a very short time, in the winter of 1348-9 the terrible plague, the Black Death, swept up from the Dorset coast, with devastating consequences for the villages and towns that lay in its path. Some places never recovered. Bentworth was at least more fortunate than that, but the next surviving rental, for about fifty years later, bears little relation to the first, silent testimony to the changes that had taken place. The number of tenancies had fallen from forty to twenty five, though the total rent had increased a little, and only one is recognisable from the previous list – that formerly held by John atte Slade at Ashley.

Happily for the history of Bentworth, Margery, the daughter of William and Matilda at the Hall, and sister of Bishop Richard, had married James Molyns of Millcourt, Binsted. Their daughter Juliana, heir to the family's land holding, is our link with the past. She became the second wife of Richard Windsor, and their son James was the heir to the Windsor, Bentworth and Millcourt properties, the records of which have survived as a basis for research.

Richard Windsor was descended from a family which had held the chief tenancy of the manor of Stanwell in Middlesex (now on the perimeter of Heathrow airport) from the Crown since the Conquest. Early generations had been Constables of Windsor Castle and Wardens of Windsor Forest, hence their name in the style of the period, de Wyndesore. Willhall on the road to Alton, and Malshanger near Basingstoke, were two other tenancies they held by rent or service to Windsor Castle. Later they acquired land in Holybourne, Isington, Froyle, Greatham and Bramshott.

The WINDSOR, BENTWORTH family connection

Walter Fitz Other,
Constable of Windsor Castle,
1086 lord of manor of Stanwell.

Seven generations who used the designation, "de Windesore".

William de Aule als. William of Bentworth Constable of Farnham Castle, d. before 1327 m. Matilda died after 1340

?William elder s.

Richard Bp. of London, d. 1339

Margery d. after 1367

m. James Molyns of Millcourt, Binsted.

Richard Windsor died 1367 married 2nd Juliana Molyns d. before 1367

James Windsor m. Elizabeth Strechie. Ipm 1372.

Miles Windsor m. Alice Wymondham.

Brian Windsor m. Alice Drewe. Ipm 1406.

Miles died 1401

Richard Windsor died 1428 m. Christian Fauconer

Miles Windsor died 1451 m. Joanne Greene

Thomas Windsor died 1485 m. Elizabeth Andrews

Andrew m. Elizabeth Blount
1467-1543
1st. Baron Windsor.

Anthony Windsor Kt.

Margaret Abbess of Sion.

Alice

George

William Windsor of Bradenham, 1499-1558 2nd. Baron Windsor.

Edmund

Thomas

4 daughters

5th son

Edward c. 1532-1574 3rd Baron Windsor.

m. Katharine d. of John Vere 16th Earl of Oxford.

Walter

m. Margaret d. of Sir Geoffrey Pole.

William

m. Eliz. d. of Wm. 3rd. E. of Worcester.

Frederick 1559-1585 4th Baron Windsor.

Henry 1562-1605 5th Baron Windsor.

m. Anne d. of Sir Thomas Rivet.

Edward d. 1599 at Tardebigge, Worcs.

Andrew

Elizabeth Windsor, widow of Juliana's son James, died in 1372 leaving an estate at Hall Farm detailed in her *Inquisition Post Mortem* as 160 acres of arable, a garden of six acres, and sixty acres of woodland, for which she paid William Melton, the lord of the manor, £7 13. 4d. a year. She rented another sixty acres belonging to the rector of Bentworth for which she paid 7s. 8d., and she also paid the lord of Bradley one penny at Michaelmas for a messuage (a house with outbuildings and a garden) at Ashley. For tenure of Holt Croft, sublet as in the past to someone in the village, she paid the Prior of the Hospital of St. John of Jerusalem in England four marks (£2 13s. 4d.), the value of four bushels of corn.

Elizabeth's son Miles Windsor was in possession of the same estate when he died in 1387 in Spain in the service of John of Gaunt, Duke of Lancaster, and claimant to the throne of Castile. So were later generations until Miles' namesake and great grandson died in 1451 in Italy on a pilgrimage to the Holy Land, and was buried in a monastery at Ferrara.

His son and heir, Thomas, had just come of age. For the next thirty-four years – some of the most turbulent in English history as they spanned the Wars of the Roses – Thomas Windsor was lord of the manor of Bentworth Hall, as Hall Farm and its lands was known. His manorial court rolls and those of his son Andrew have survived as a most useful series covering fifty-four years from 1477, and among the entries are the distant echoes of the village we know today.

> 1478. To this court came William Weller and took from the lord one messuage . . . 26 acres of arable in the fields of Bentworth . . . and Swaynes Croft . . .

Swaynes Croft today is a bumpy hollow just inside the gate to Dunstalls Field in Drury Lane, but some can remember an old farm house of a later period that stood there until 1947. William was there for about twenty years. In 1528 we pick up the early history of Weller's Farm on its present site. At a court held on the Feast of St. Clement (November 23rd) William Weller, probably the son of the first William, took from the lord a tenement with a garden and an adjoining close, previously called White's, a pittel called Pykes, another called Battisfords, and 26 acres in the fields.

From the same court record of 1478 East End emerges as a settlement of three established farmsteads. John Stacy took from the lord a messuage and 36 acres, together with Mill Purrock and Battisfords Crofts. By 1550 the holding was in the hands of Thomas Gunner, and it was probably his son Robert who built the house we now know as Greensleeves. Stacy's neighbour at East End Farm was John Gover, and across the road at East End House was John Barber, tenant of the land which is now part of Summerley.

The records reveal too how the old system of the open fields was changing. In addition to the 160 acres belonging to Hall Farm which were leased by the Windsors to a tenant farmer, the rest of the tenants between them had at least another 400 acres. Originally these fields had been divided into strips, following general practice, and allotted to the lord and his tenants. But in the course of centuries, as the holdings changed hands, some of these strips were joined together as blocks of land; others were extended by taking in bordering grazing land.

Further closes, crofts and purrocks were clearings made along the tracks through the woods which were enclosed and let to tenants, as happened for example along Holt Lane, first recorded in 1493.

Some enclosures, however, were not acceptable to the tenants. At a court in 1487 the men complained that a farmer who leased his holding from John Melton, the chief lord, had encroached and imparked the land of the lord of Bentworth Hall, Andrew Windsor, which had been part of their common pasture. Threats to their vital grazing land arose too in another form in 1499 when they complained that the same farmer and two others had overstocked the common pasture with twenty seven pigs. The culprits were fined for each animal in excess of their grazing right.

The common pasture, downland and woodland, almost encircled the parish as far as the boundaries to similar areas of the neighbouring villages. The Holt stretched from the edge of South Field through Colliers Wood to Hackett Hill at Wivelrod and along the Medstead boundary to a ditch which divided it from Fellingdean.

Fellingdean, recalled in the field names Feldens and Veldens, was the summer cow pasture which extended from Mucklands to Ashley and the Medstead and Wield boundaries. Haileydean lay to the north across the valley towards Burkham and the Lasham boundary. The Saxon element in the names, holt for wood, dean or *den* for pasture, suggests that the grazing system could have been as old as the settlements. For the tenants of Burkham there was also the large common where the boundaries of Bentworth, Bradley, Herriard and Lasham met.

Despite the provision and regulation of grazing, many, if not most of the villagers, probably lived precariously close to subsistence level. Some had only ten acres, or even less, in the fields; none except the leaseholders had more than fifty acres, with a close or croft attached to their small farmstead. If they were cottagers, they might have had only a garden, where they could grow vegetables, some fruit, and pen a pig or a sheep which they fattened on the common or wayside verges. To add to the rigours of life there were frequent reports in the manor court of the ruinous condition of the houses. It seems probable that the lord's steward was not authorising the felling of trees necessary for the repair of the timber framed houses and barns, and that there was an insufficient supply of thatching straw in the village.

The Village During the Reformation

It seems that Thomas Windsor was a member of the court of Edward IV, for when the king died suddenly, and preparations had to be made quickly for the coronation of his young son Edward V, Thomas was among those nominated to receive the Order of the Bath. But of course there was no coronation: Edward and his brother were the Princes in the Tower, and never seen again. The country had suffered almost a hundred years of plots and counter plots, murder and sudden changes of power, and few men knew with certainty to whom they owed their loyalty. Thomas Windsor as Constable of Windsor Castle, the appointment held by his forbears under the Norman kings, saw it as his duty to follow the banner of King Richard to Bosworth Field. He died a month later of wounds sustained in the battle, just a day or two after being pardoned by the victorious Henry Tudor, now Henry VII.

Andrew, elder son and heir of Thomas Windsor, was a young man barely out of his teens, training to be a lawyer. At the age of thirty he was a Bencher of Middle Temple, and a few years later he became Keeper of the Great Wardrobe, not a domestic office, as the title might suggest, but the ancient title of an accounting department of the royal household. Re-appointed by Henry VIII on his accession, Andrew Windsor remained within the close circle of the royal court until he died in 1543. His activities and duties, as recorded in the State Papers were many and various. He was with the king in the French campaign of 1512, and later at the Field of the Cloth of Gold. There were also the unspectacular commissions: to survey the navy in the Thames, to report on the problems arising from the increasing number of parks in the countryside, to sit as a judge in London and the shires. When M.P. for Buckinghamshire in 1529, he was raised to the peerage as the first Baron Windsor of Stanwell, to help the balance of power in the Upper House during the momentous Reformation Parliament. It was a long career in the service of the Crown, and yet in the end Henry, in one of those unpredictable turns of mood which characterised his later years, demanded the one thing that Andrew Windsor prized, his ancestral home, the manor of Stanwell. Andrew died a fortnight after the deeds were signed making it over to the king, in 1543.

There are so many links in Hampshire and Surrey with Andrew Windsor and his family that he cannot have been a stranger to the village. On the other hand, he was probably never more than a much respected visitor, occupying occasionally and briefly the upper rooms of Hall Farm. There was probably one such occasion in 1510 when he was sitting as a judge in Winchester with Sir Guy Palmes, a king's serjeant at law. It was about the time that John Melton, lord of the manor of Bentworth, died leaving an heir under age. Palmes, who was of Yorkshire stock like Melton, was interested in the Hampshire land market and persuaded the Melton family to sell. Thus Palmes became the new lord of Bentworth, the first change for two hundred years, and as it transpired, of some consequence to the village.

The advowson of the church at Bentworth (that is, the right to present a rector to the living) had belonged to the lord of the manor since the charter of 1165, and at the end of 1511 the living became vacant on the death of Nicholas Makyn, rector both of Bentworth and of Lasham where he lived. A chaplain was appointed; but his place was soon taken by one John Palmes, obviously a member of the new lord's family, but the exact relationship is not known. He remained the rector for more than twenty years, becoming an increasingly outspoken Protestant preacher, as rural dean of Alton, at a time when the content of sermons could have considerable political implications. Such behaviour would have given no pleasure to the prominent members of his family, who remained strong Catholics. Early in 1539 matters came to a head when Stephen Gardiner, Bishop of Winchester, deprived him of the living.

Palmes was a victim of the struggle then at its height between the old Catholic Church led by Gardiner, recently returned to England after a spell of diplomatic duty abroad, and Thomas Cromwell, the king's chief minister and vicar-general of the newly created Church of England. Summoned to appear before the Consistory Court on the disciplinary charge of being married, Palmes appealed to Cromwell for help, declaring that he had not taken a vow of celibacy, and that the King's patent did not forbid marriage. But it was of no avail. In November the King had made known by proclamation that his religious views were unchanged despite the break with Rome, and that among the matters at issue he specifically forbade the marriage of clergy. By the end of the year Cromwell had committed the King to the disastrous marriage with Anne of Cleves, and was now desperate to retain his influence at Court, where the Duke of Norfolk and Bishop Gardiner were gaining the ascendancy. So Cromwell, who could be very dilatory when it suited his purpose, let Gardiner have his way. Indeed he may have known that the former abbot Thomas Stephens, who had so accommodatingly surrendered first Netley Abbey and then Beaulieu to his Commissioners, was to be the next incumbent of Bentworth, and so had some reason for letting matters take their course.

A month after the Consistory Court hearing, to the clamour of jangled bells, Palmes was ejected from his church by the Sheriff's men and the doors of the tithe barn locked. Stephens moved into the rectory with one or two of his monks, and in the course of the next few years invested his money in land in Alton. Ironically a codicil to his will eventually revealed that he had left the land in trust for his daughter! Palmes after his forcible removal, made one last fruitless appeal to Cromwell from the house to which he retired at Monk Sherborne. Four years later he at least died in his bed, leaving a wife and three young sons. Cromwell on the other hand, engaged in the deadly game of Tudor politics, paid the ultimate forfeit on the scaffold of Tower Green, little more than a year after the disturbance in Bentworth.

In 1550 on the death of Stephens, the lord of the manor, by then Sir Francis Palmes, recovered the right to the advowson of the church, and resolving in those uncertain times to retain control and derive some profit from his grandfather's investment, leased the rectory to his brother. This was Thomas Palmes, a layman, who lived in the village and farmed the land for almost fifty years. On his death the lease was handed on in turn to younger members of the family until shortly before the Civil War. Thus the value of the living to the incumbent was reduced, a frequent complaint of Protestant reformers throughout the country, for it led to pluralism and poorly educated clergy.

The fifty or so families living in the village do not seem to have been swayed by John Palmes' Protestant teaching. They continued to leave money in their wills for masses to be said for their souls, for the maintenance of the rood and its light, and for the lights before the images of the Virgin, St. Thomas and St. Nicholas. Only when such images were forbidden by the Council of Edward VI did they begin to change their ways. In 1552 John Willway of Burkham made his will in the new form with a generous gift of eight pence to every poor household in Bentworth, Wield and Ellisfield, and bequests, mostly of sheep, to his family, friends, and god-children. His friends valued his goods and chattels at £12 14s. 4d., including one hundred and twenty sheep at £10.

The inventory of the church three months later lists two chalices and patens, a number of vestments and a surplice, an altar cloth, three bells in the tower, a sanctus bell and a hand bell, a pair of censers, a pair of lead candlesticks, and a gilded copper crucifix which Nicholas Makyn had given to the church. Evidently the church wardens had yet to obtain a copy of the new prayer book and a bible, and twelve months more delay could have seen them safely through the next five years of the ruthless turnaround policy of Mary Tudor.

Inconspicuous villagers were spared the worst effects of the religious turmoil, but the Windsor family, known to be steadfast Catholics were in greater peril. In the early years of Elizabeth's reign Edward, the third baron, was still being appointed to Commissions, and in 1566 entertained the Queen at his home in Bradenham, near Wycombe, Buckinghamshire, on her way back from Oxford. But from 1568, while Mary, Queen of Scots remained imprisoned in England and the centre of conspiracies, Catholics in general were viewed with growing suspicion as a threat to the Queen, the State and the Established church. Edward went into exile, and died in Germany in 1574. His last request was that his heart should be brought back to England to be buried beneath the tomb of his father in the chapel at Bradenham. A year later, perhaps to encourage them to take their

Henry, 5th Baron Windsor.
Painted in 1588 when he was 26.

place at court, two of his sons, Frederick, his heir barely sixteen, and Henry were commanded by the Queen to carry the Order of the Garter to Henry III of France. Did they, Catholics, know that their mission was to confirm the Treaty of Blois negotiated by the Protestant envoy, Francis Walsingham? And who suggested them as the messengers?

Frederick went on to become a master of the courtly arts of the tournament in the company of such exponents as Sir Philip Sydney, Fulke Greville, and the Earl of Arundel. But the heavy fines his family had been paying and continued to pay as recusants were draining their financial resources. By the time his brother Henry succeeded to the barony in 1585, many of their estates had been sold. Bentworth, the last in Hampshire, was sold in 1590 to Robert Hunt whose family had been their tenants at Hall Farm for a hundred years or more.

In 1603 as the Tudor monarchy passed into history Nicholas Holdip reported to his bishop that there were one hundred and eighty five communicants in the parish, no recusants, but five non-communicants. Five years later in the winter of 1608 the old church was all but destroyed. At the Epiphany Quarter Sessions it was reported that the church at Bentworth "hath been burnt and utterlie ruined by fire happening by lightning from Heaven". The parishioners could be forgiven some exaggeration if, as is probable, they were left with a blackened roofless shell. But at least they saved the font cover "given by Martha Hunt Anno 1605", the wife of Robert Hunt of Hall Place, then the lord of the manor. Nicholas Holdip was spared the distress of seeing his church burn. He died in 1606, and his stone memorial erected by his wife survives today on the chancel wall.

New Houses in the Stuart Village

When Robert Hunt bought the manor of Bentworth Hall in 1590 he stretched his resources to the limit to keep Hall Farm where his family had lived for so long, but only as tenants, and were to stay, as it turned out, for almost another hundred years. Within a month of the purchase he had sold a large area of West Field and the land to the north of Ashley called Bullfields, with common rights for 'one hundred sheep and all manner of other beasts' to a Berkshire investor. By the end of the year he had sold a large estate at Burkham to Robert Magewick, a clothier in Alton who came from a Hampshire farming background. This land had been leased for many years by the Willway family just as the Hunts had leased Hall Farm. In fact John Willway had paid the highest tax in the village to Henry VIII's Great Subsidy of 1524, and the hamlet had enjoyed a largely independent existence with its own field system, common grazing, and woodlands. It was this land which the Magewick family and their descendants the Battins and the Coulthards, whose memorials are in the church, farmed until late in the nineteenth century.

Robert Hunt held his first manor court at Hall Farm in April 1590 when the tenants did fealty to their new lord and paid him the customary silver penny for their lands. Among those tenants was a relative newcomer to the village, George Wither, younger son of Richard Wither of Manydown, Wootton St. Lawrence, who had married Mary Hunt of Thedden. They set up home at first in East End House, rented from William Hinwood, and while the country was preparing its defences against the Spanish Armada in June 1588, their first child was born, and named after his father. Two more sons survived into manhood – James, who became Mayor of Basingstoke, and Anthony, an innkeeper in Alresford – and four daughters.

The immediate need of George Wither senior was to obtain land, and here his interest in surveying, unusual for those days, probably helped. Within a year he had bought a messuage with an acre of land called Pykes, and ten acres in the fields. He built a cottage, still standing, on the land called Pykes, and sold it to a certain John Turner. He also acquired three other tenancies which put together gave him a large acreage in the fields, as well as grazing rights on the commons and small meadows in the centre of the village. Here on the land between Church Street and the High Street he built a house now called Hunts Cottage and a farmstead. By the time of his death in 1629 he was one of the wealthiest farmers in the village, with a herd of dairy cattle, a flock of thirty ewes, (kept more for their milk than their wool) and two fattenning and sixteen lean hogs (which were partly fed on the whey from the milk). On November 19th when his friends valued his goods for probate, seven hundredweight of cheese, two hundred pounds of butter, thirty bushels of apples, and three tods (84 lbs) of wool were stored in the lofts. Hanging in the bakehouse were seven hogs of bacon; in the barn he had wheat, barley, oats and peas, and out in the fields twenty three acres of wheat had been sown ready for next season.

When his father died the younger George had been living in London for twenty years. Like many sons of country gentlemen he had received his early education from private tutors, in his case two men of undoubted ability. The first, Ralph Starkey, a distant relative by marriage, was keenly interested in historical documents and collected them avidly. Eventually part of his collection was bought by Sir Edward Harley and became the core of the Harleian Manuscripts now in the British Library. Preserved with them are two of Starkey's own works, a long poem in the style of Edmund Spenser, and a treatise on 'The Privilege and Practice of the High Court of Parliament'. His second tutor was John Greaves, rector of Colemore, less than ten miles from Bentworth. Three of his sons became eminent in their spheres: John, the eldest, a mathematician, became Professor of Astronomy at Oxford, the second, Edward who studied medicine in Amsterdam, was knighted when court physician to Charles II, while Thomas achieved fame as an orientalist. Greaves' pupils would have been well grounded in latin and greek because the textbooks of most subjects were still the ancient classics. From these foundations George grew up to translate the latin psalms in to

English verse, and write veiled political criticism in the code of allegories and mythology. His appreciation of Edmund Spenser's verse was formed very early, not just by Starkey, but perhaps by his father. Spenser stayed in Alton for a short time, probably in 1596, to escape the plague in London, while he was writing the later parts of the *Faerie Queene*. As the son of a London cloth merchant, what could be more natural than that he should be entertained by some of the wealthy clothiers and educated gentlemen farmers in and around Alton? According to legend he lived in a house in Amery Street near the Market Place; a possible alternative would be Lady Ursula Walsingham's rectory on Amery Hill. He had been staying in the house of her daughter the Countess of Essex in London.

After two years at Magdalen College, Oxford, where George wrote the haunting 'I loved a lass, a fair one,' with its chorus 'But now alas! she's left me, Falero, lero, loo.' he returned home to help his father, and continued to write his lyrical verse, and so, 'finding that mere countrie business was not my calling', he moved to London to study law. There he found the company he needed in the bookshops round St. Paul's, the taverns in Fleet Street and the Strand, and soon the patronage of the Court at Whitehall, a world rich in legal and literary gossip, political and religious debate.

In 1611 when he was only twenty three, he published his first edition of *Abuses Stript and Whipt*, a satirical comment on human frailties and natural ambitions. It was popularly received and protected by the patronage of the Princess Elizabeth, daughter of James I. But by the time he produced another edition she was in Germany married to the Elector Palatine, and the government, sensitive to the mildest criticism, found an excuse to cast him into the Marshalsea Prison. Eventually the Earl of Pembroke succeeded in obtaining his release, and in 1615 George entered Lincoln's Inn. Nevertheless he continued to write his allegorical verse which could be read at more than one level of understanding. Inevitably he found himself in prison again until fortunately his translations of the psalms won the praise of James I. As a reward he was granted a patent that all psalters should include his *Hymns and Songs of the Church*, as a first English hymnal. However it did him little good as the printing trade resented the monopoly and would not print for him. In later years when he was much more seriously minded,

George Wither, by John Payne.

Wither despised his early pastoral poems, but for this reader they remain his memorable work.

Hidden in the lines of *Fair Virtue* is a long description of Bentworth as he knew it, a lad of eighteen walking the downs with his father's sheep, and quenching his thirst with the shepherds at 'the well below the town' – Down Well, as it was later known, in the valley in front of the present Well Cottages.

> The pleasant way as up those hills you climb,
> Is strewed o'er with marjoram and thyme,
> Which grows unset. The hedgerows do not want
> The cowslip, violet, primrose, nor a plant
> That freshly scents, as birch doth green and tall;
> Low sallows, on whose blooming bees do fall;
> Fair woodbines, which about the hedges twine;
> Smooth privet, and the sharp, sweet eglantine;
> With many more, whose leaves and blossoms fair
> The earth adorn and oft perfume the air.
> When you into the highest do attain,
> An admixture both of wood and plain
> You shall behold, which, though aloft it lie,
> Hath downs for sheep and fields for husbandry.
> So much, at least, as little needeth more,
> If not enough to merchandise their store.
> In every row hath Nature planteth there
> Some banquet for the hungry passenger.
> For here the hazel-nut and filbert grows;
> There bulloes, and a little further sloes;
> On this hand standeth a fair wilding-tree;
> On that large thickets of black cherries be.
> The shrubby fields are raspice-orchards there,
> The new-fell'd woods like strawberry gardens are;
> And had the king of rivers blest those hills
> With some small number of such pretty rills
> As flow elsewhere, Arcadia had not seen
> A sweeter plot of earth than this had been.

Wither had begun *Fair Virtue* in 1606 as a pleasant past-time, and did not publish it until 1622, a year significant in the history of

Bentworth, when his remembrance of the open downs may have been brought to mind. In that year the lords and tenants came to an agreement for the enclosure of the commons. In particular the Holt, Fellingdean, Haileydean, and the downs between Childer Hill and the Shalden boundary, were to be shared out between them in proportion to their grazing rights. A memory of the past lingers in the names of some of the fields created at this time, Hunt's Common, Feldens, Great Down, the three fields of Haileydean, and others which were mapped and recorded in the Tithe Award of 1840. The agreement was probably welcomed by both sides. Edward Nevill, who had bought the chief manor of Bentworth from his father in law, Sir Guy Palmes, in 1616, would benefit like Robert Hunt from the larger land market, and the tenants would have greater freedom to follow the farming practice of their choice. Moreover we may assume, George Wither the elder, a surveyor, was there to help them – the right man in the right place at the right time. The agreement appears to have been an early example of enclosure in the area. Heydown in Alton had been enclosed a few years earlier, and Lasham soon after, but Stancombe and Soldridge Commons in Medstead were not enclosed until 1735, and then by Act of Parliament.

These years were notable too as the time when more than a dozen of the houses admired in the village today were built, part of the 'Great Rebuilding' movement observed in other areas of the country. In 1585 the tenants had taken Lord Frederick Windsor to the Chancery Court for an affirmation of their rights – among other things to 'top, lop, and cut down trees growing upon their tenements, to pull down and re-edify their houses at will'. They had to repeat the process in 1607 in a complaint against Robert Hunt, but new building was already under way by then.

Timber-framed at first, later in brick, most of the new houses had the same distinctive ground plan, though they have since been extended and modernised almost beyond recognition. The principal feature was a thick chimney stack, slightly off centre, serving two fireplaces back to back. There was one room one side, and on the other side a room with another smaller unheated room leading off it. The front entrance opened into a lobby at one side of the stack, with a door to right and left, and a staircase generally very narrow and twisting, rose up the side of the stack at the other end. Architectural historians sometimes refer to the style as lobby entrance houses.

The hamlet of Holt Lane End began to take shape on the edge of the common in these years, and the three original houses, all built to this plan, are still standing. The court roll of 1600 records that Thomas Tilboroe and his wife Helen had bought a parcel of land called Holt Close of four acres and three roods. Tilboroe, who had been working for Thomas Palmes, had been left on his master's death in 1597, a score of wether sheep, his great black travelling gelding and two kyne, to give him a start on his own. The names of his neighbours in the other two houses were found in the parish register. At first the new settlement was known as "att wood" when in 1603 Nicholas Holdip recorded that he had christened Joan, the daughter of "William Hunt att Wood", and in 1617 his successor John Powell baptised a son of William Gregory. By the 1620s the families of all three men were described as living at "Holt Lane". William Hunt's house is now Holt Cottage, and that of William Gregory forms the core of Holt Green. Even in 1800 the track in front of the house was still called Gregory's Lane, though the family had sold it as long ago as 1658. Within a few years a fourth cottage was built by William Hall beside the longer lane leading to Colliers Wood near Tilboroe's; but it was demolished about a hundred years ago and the land taken into the surrounding field.

The new settlement at Holt Lane End was only a few hundred yards from the site of the old Hospitallers' tenement at Holt Croft, and there a very pleasing and surprising example of continuity has been found. During conversion work at Yew Tree Cottage the stripping of plaster from a seemingly nineteenth century extension revealed two gable ends side by side. An eighteenth century flint addition had been made to a seventeenth century brick lobby plan house, and the valley between the two roof lines bricked across in the nineteenth century to support a low-pitched slate roof. The lobby plan house built about 1660 was the home of William Ballchild and his wife Alice. He described himself as a husbandman, but was a comfortably placed small farmer with goods and bonds to the value of £136 at the time of his death in 1692. The inventory described the house as consisting of a hall (by then sometimes called a parlour), kitchen and buttery, and up the stairs, a lodging chamber. There was still corn in the barn in February, and his winter sowing had been done. Seventeen sheep were out in the field, and a cow and two hogs in a gateroom, which suggests that some of the old buildings were still standing. He held the land on a three hundred years lease from the lord of the manor of Godsfield, a lease probably granted before 1550 to the Gosden family who were the village wheelwrights. The old trade came back to the place in the nineteenth century, largely because of the pond at the bend in the road, and again in association with a small farm, known oddly in view of its history, as New Place Farm.

There was a small meadow, little more than a quarter of an acre, beside the pond, which belonged to Robert Compton – hence the name of Comptons for the much larger field there today, and for the modern houses near the site. Robert was a cottager listed among nine of that status in the court roll of 1625, but he is the only one who has been identified. His home, now the site of Rose Cottage, was nearer to the centre of the village on a piece of waste between the track of Holt Lane and the old field boundary. A century later the cottage was rebuilt in flint and brick, and in 1836 extended as the date tablet indicates by George Bone, who belonged to a family of local blacksmiths. The neighbouring house, "Andrews", is of the same period and built to the lobby plan, and as the court roll of 1645 and 1646 relates, was "set up .... upon the waste" without licence by Jerome North. No court had been held since 1635 so the house may have been in existence for almost ten years, including the three years of civil war. He admitted the offence and was granted a pardon on payment of one silver penny and a yearly rent of one capon to the lord on the Feast Day of the Nativity, commuted to one shilling.

Lobby plan houses were built too at Ashley and Wivelrod, but as replacements within the existing settlements. However, on part of the newly enclosed common land close to the Medstead boundary at New Copse, a new house of the same style was built remote from the old settlements. By the beginning of the nineteenth century it had become a one hundred acres farm, then called New Coppice, and now Medstead Grange, but not until this century were other houses built on the neighbouring land. The original site was bought by John Brokett, a minister of probably Calvinist persuasion, early in the 1640s. From snippets of information it appears that he was one of many driven out of Essex by Laudian persecution, most of whom emigrated to North America. But Brokett was offered a lectureship to preach at Basingstoke and that seems to have brought him into

Hampshire. His arrival in Bentworth was timely as parson Timothy Hood had been deprived of the living, like the vicar of Alton, and forced to leave the village. In his absence Brokett unofficially brought comfort as a "faithful pastor" to the villagers in their hour of need, as Martin Hide wrote on his death bed in 1647.

Little else is known about the village during the Civil War, but it cannot have escaped the hardships of being in an area bounded by the three strongholds of Winchester, Farnham and Basing House. Sir Humphrey Bennett of Shalden was recruiting men for his Royalist regiment, Colonel Richard Norton, a member of the old Rotherfield family, commanded the Parliamentary horse. In the autumn of 1643 the Royalists were quartered in Alton and Alresford, and Farnham was the headquarters of the Parliamentary Southern Army. Foraging parties roamed the countryside far and wide for food and fodder, horses and carts, and supplies of all kinds; crops were ruined, livestock stolen, to the near destitution of everyone. Alton fell to Sir William Waller's Parliamentary army on December 13th 1643, after a fight through the streets to the churchyard, and a last heroic stand by Colonel Boles and his men in the parish church, which still bears the scars of the battle. In the following March Lord Hopton's Royalists were caught in the undulating country and narrow lanes round Cheriton and cut to pieces. The battle proved to be one of the turning points in the war. In October 1645 Winchester surrendered to Cromwell, and three days later Basing House was overwhelmed.

The war moved away to the north and west, until eventually the King was checked in all directions. He chose to surrender to the Scots and was imprisoned at Newcastle. For nearly a year he refused on the one hand the Scots demand that Presbyterianism be imposed in England, and on the other, Parliament's demand for the abolition of the Established Church. In February 1647 Parliament paid off the Scots army, and the King was brought south to Hampton Court. For a time there was a chance of an agreement, but the moment passed. By November Cromwell had lost control of the army, and the King, fearful for his life, slipped away to Carisbrooke Castle in the Isle of Wight. Yet very quickly the scene changed; Cromwell back at the head of his army stormed across the country crushing all opposition, until in December 1648 there was only the King, by now imprisoned at Hurst Castle. Those people who saw the King riding back to London through Alresford and Alton, under the escort of a hundred armed officers and men, are unlikely to have forgotten the experience. Little more than a month later, on January 30th, he was beheaded in front of the Banqueting House in Whitehall. Twelve years of puritanical misgovernment followed before his son Charles II was welcomed back to England and the throne in May 1660.

Soon after the Restoration a new form of taxation was introduced, the Hearth Tax, and the surviving returns provide some indication of the size of the village at the time. Twenty eight householders are listed, including one exempt on grounds of poverty. It seems that a blind eye was turned to perhaps a dozen more whose names appear in other records but the parish officers thought should be omitted for the same reason, making a total of say forty. This surprisingly is nine less than had been assessed to contribute to Henry VIII's Great Subsidy of 1524. The bishop's returns of 1603 and 1676 also suggest that the population figure did not increase over that period, but remained constant at between 190 and 192 communicants. Yet the fact that new houses were built at Holt Lane End shows that there was a demand for housing. The first new houses there were built by the sons of families who had been tenants for a hundred years or more, and held land in the common fields and the new enclosures. All three complied with the act of 1589 which required that a new cottage should have four acres attached to it, enough it was thought to ensure the family did not become a charge on the poor rate. The other houses on the waste were put up by labourers who either had a claim to a small piece of land like Comptons, or intended by further encroachment to extend the garden to produce food and so eke out their wages, as Jerome North succeeded in part in doing. Some he had to return to the waste.

Another source of information, the series of probate inventories covering the years 1550 – 1700, suggest an improving standard of living. The houses, whether new, rebuilt, or with an added 'new hall', were more comfortably furnished, with a chair or two, and stools, in addition to the usual table and form. There were more household utensils, and most people had at least some pewter dishes. In the chamber it became usual to find a feather bed upon a bedstead and flock mattress, with sheets, blankets and a coverlet, and chests, instead of a coffer or a trunk, for clothes and linen.

Where in the early years of the inventories £26 was an average valuation and £50 the maximum, in the last forty years, although there were some smallholders whose goods amounted to less than £20, the average had risen to £138, just about equal to the rate of inflation. The highest surviving valuation was £460, the sum total of the goods and chattels of William Hunt, yeoman, of East End House in September 1682. He had a hundred and forty sheep, eleven cows and bullocks, and forty pigs, valued together at £79. His six horses, two waggons, two dung carts, five harrows, the plough and all the harness came to £60. The corn in the barns was valued at £180, and his seed wheat at £9. There was wool in the loft valued at £29, and bacon worth £3 on a rack in the kitchen. If one adds £72 out on loan, his farming enterprise accounted for £432 (94%) of his total estate. Compared with the valuations of clothiers and maltsters in Alton, or some other farmers in the area, it was not a big total, but in Bentworth it was exceptional.

Unfortunately no inventories have been found for Robert Hunt and his family at Hall Place farm, or the Magewicks at Burkham, to provide an insight into the scale and nature of their farming as members of the rising gentry class. Fifty years earlier when George Wither, the elder, gentleman, had died his estate had been valued at £340, of which his farming activity accounted for less than half his worldly goods. There were books and his measuring instruments in "the study", carpets and cushions in the hall, table cloths and fine napkins among the linen, and twenty great pewter platters for the table. As his son wrote, somewhat boastfully to our ears, but in tune with the times,

> "When daily I on change of dainties fed,
> Lodged night by night upon an easy bed
> In lordly chambers, and had wherewithall
> Attendants forwarder than I to call
> Who brought me all things needful: when at hand
> Hounds, hawks and horses were at my command."
> *Britain's Remembrancer,* 1628.

New Land Owners

The financial problems of the Windsors and Robert Hunt which had surfaced in 1590 were experienced also by Edward Nevill. The agreement in 1622 to enclose the commons revealed that Nevill was in partnership with John Terry, a goldsmith in the City of London, and his brother Thomas Terry farming at Long Sutton, six miles from Bentworth. Also, Robert Hunt had handed over his manor rights, at least for the time being, to Sir James Wolveridge, a lawyer in Odiham. In 1651 the survivors of these alliances, Thomas Terry, the Wolveridge family, and Robert Hunt, probably by now the son, contracted for the eventual transfer of the manor to Thomas Turgis, citizen and grocer of London. In the meantime Robert was to continue farming at Hall Place for life, and did fealty, as lord once more of the manor of Bentworth Hall, to Thomas Terry, lord of the manor of Bentworth. So fortunately some semblance of continuity was maintained in the village during the turmoil of the Civil War and Interregnum. Another twenty years passed before Robert died at the fine age of 79 in 1671.

For his first court held the following May Thomas Turgis, esquire, as now he was known, instructed a well-known barrister as his steward, Arthur Bold, Member of Parliament for Petersfield, enough in itself to suggest that Turgis was a man of substance and influence. He was also a generous man. In his will, proved in 1705, he left ten pounds to the poor of each parish where he had property (£70 in all), and one hundred pounds each to St. Bartholomew's Hospital and St. Thomas's, and to Christ's Hospital "for the poor boys and girls brought up and educated there". The manor of Bentworth he left to a friend Thomas Urry of Gatcombe in the Isle of Wight, who seems to have shown little, if any, interest in the village.

Meanwhile in 1677 a new farm, to be known as Corporation,

and later Powells Farm, consisting of two hundred and forty six acres of the former common land, had been bought by the Mayor and Corporation of Basingstoke as trustees of the Richard Aldworth Charity. The tenant was John Henwood who, it seems, was in possession of Edward Nevill's former manor farmstead – identified by a dovecot among its outbuildings. Henwood probably rebuilt the house, which kept his name until the late nineteenth century; and today it is Ivalls on the corner of the village green. Its 17th century connections suggest that it may have been the site of the Melton's medieval manor farmstead as well as that of Thomas Palmes.

Other questions however cannot be answered. At a time when the manor system ceased to function, and two of the large estates were owned by outsiders, it is unfortunate that the parish records have been lost. Undoubtedly the farmers performed their accustomed duties as church wardens and poor law overseers, but there is nothing to identify the farmer at Hall Farm for fifty years, for example. That is a pity because for nine months in 1729 – 30 the game keeper brought terror to the village and threatened the lives of people in Alton and as far away as Alice Holt Forest. The details of this bizarre episode have been found by E.P. Thompson and published in his book *Whigs and Hunters: the Origin of the Black Act*.

The gamekeeper was Lewis Gunner who came of old village stock, though he was born in Holybourne where his father had been a maltster. By 1729 he was in his late fifties and according to various comments, very obnoxious, insolent and ill-tempered. He always carried loaded pistols and acted "with great severity, by shooting gentlemen's and farmers' dogs, and taking guns and nets from such as were not qualified". Even worse he was known to discharge his pistols deliberately to frighten opponents. In June 1729 he went too far; he fired at an opponent "in a public room in Alton". Fortunately the bullet lodged in the wall, allowing Gunner to claim he had not aimed at the man. But the circumstances were such that he was arrested, examined by Thomas Bates, a local J.P. and sent to Winchester Gaol to await the next Assizes. That night fires were started in Bentworth, in Drury Lane, which destroyed Widow Eyres' barn and part of her house and her son's, together with the barn of her neighbour Widow Gregory. It was generally accepted that Gunner's associates were responsible. A month later when Gunner was found guilty and condemned to be hanged, two barns belonging to Thomas Westbrook were burnt down, and the eaves of Widow Eyres' house again set alight, but this time the fire was put out before it got a hold. A week later, on the morning Gunner was due to be hanged, another barn was destroyed along with two adjoining houses. In a village of thatched roofs, timber framed buildings, and rick yards, the strain was intolerable. As the rector Edward Acton wrote to the Duke of Bolton at Hackwood, "My Lord I most humbly beseech your Grace to consider what a deplorable condition we are in, our farmers, labourers and servants are all worn out with toil, fear and watching . . . we are all under the dreadful apprehension of having our houses and barns fired . . . of our corn being consumed". Nonetheless there was general relief for the sake of Gunner's many relations, among them a farmer in the village, when it was known that Gunner had been reprieved, – provided he was transported, and his sentence no further reduced. On Michaelmas day, September 29th, he was released, but on condition that he *transport himself* for fourteen years. There was no police force to enforce such an order, and in early March he was still at large in the area collecting signatures to a petition for a full pardon from people too frightened to refuse. The county justices had had enough. A spokesman was sent to London with a clear message for the Secretary of State, the Duke of Newcastle, and some action, probably clandestine and unrecorded, must have been taken as nothing more was heard of Gunner and his gang.

The earliest surviving map for any part of the village is an estate map of Wivelrod drawn for Thomas Knight of Chawton in 1742. It is a charming piece of work done by Knight's agent, Edward Randall, but exists only as two copies on aged and fragile tracing paper. Since the early 16th century a younger branch of the Hunt family at Hall Place had farmed the old freehold tenement, and in 1635 it was sold to John Knight with about one hundred and sixty acres of land. The farmhouse marked A on the map is still standing, divided into two cottages, but as a result of 19th century alterations, its early origins are hardly discernible. The tell-tale string course under the rendering provided a first clue. For many years the Andrews family were the tenant farmers, and stayed on when in 1840 Edward Austen Knight agreed to sell it to John Wood of Thedden Grange. He was a wealthy retired worsted spinner from

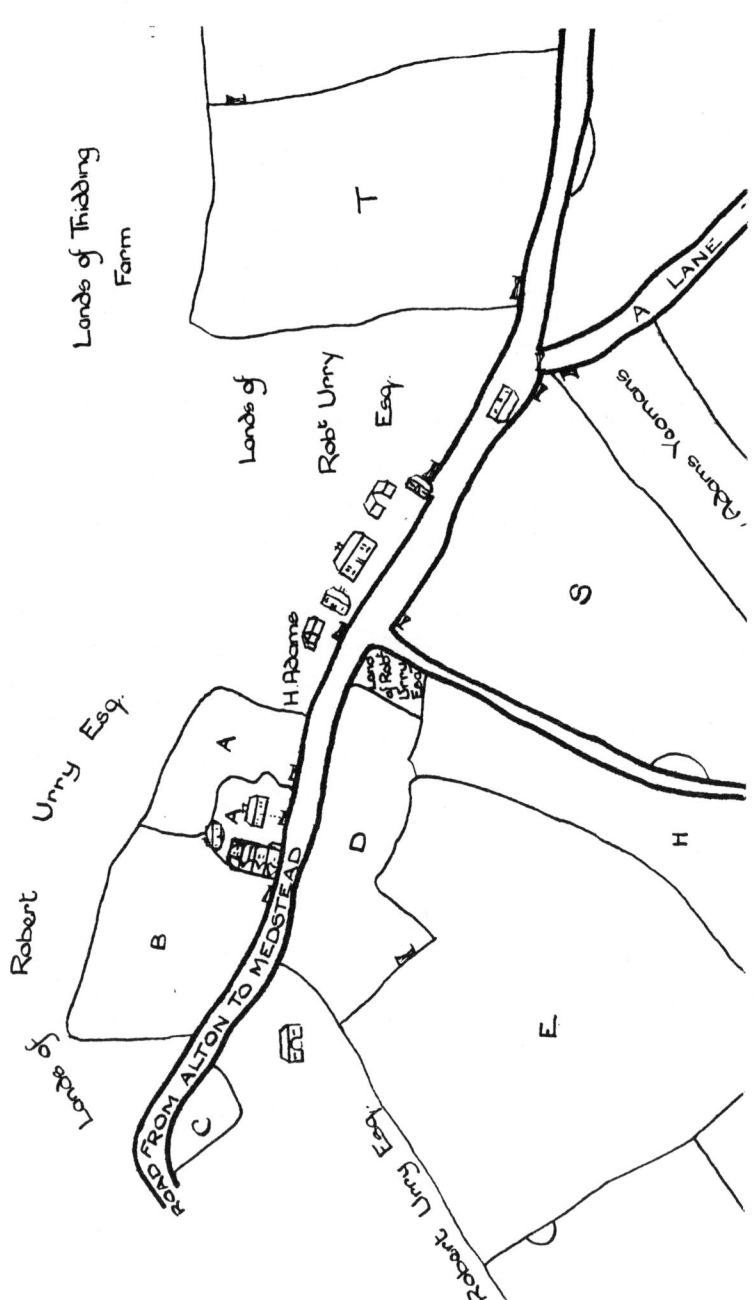

Detail from the Map of Wivelrod Farm, 1742, part of the Estate of Thomas Knight Esq.

Bradford who very soon acquired Amery, Anstey, Aylesfield and Shalden Manor farms. An Evangelical Christian, he is still honoured in Yorkshire as one of the leaders in the campaign for the Ten Hours Bill to regulate the working hours of children in the textile mills. Local business men, like Henry Hall, the Alton brewer and banker, recognised the force of his influence and sought his support in their enterprises. But for Wood's knowledge of the City and standing in this part of Hampshire, the extension of the railway from Alton to Winchester, blocked by the London and South Western Board, would never have been built.

The group of buildings marked on the map as belonging to Henry Adams, yeoman, included two houses which had been the homes of Edward and Henry Adams, brothers a generation earlier. Another piece of Hunt land, it had been divided and sold in the 1620s. In 1625 Robert Hunt had sold forty acres to John Kettlewell and sometime, perhaps about the time of the Restoration, his son Timothy had built the brick house with thatched roof, now The Old Farmhouse, which looks across the fields in the valley to the village. A few years later his widow sold the small farm to the first of several generations of the Adams family. A hundred years further on in 1766 it was sold to John Spencer, a farmer from Chawton and it remained with his family until the 1960s. At that time the house built on the lobby plan had not been altered, even to the ladder up to the attic rooms. In the front garden of the house, which is on land six hundred and fifty feet above sea level, there was a well which over the years had been taken down to the great depth of between three and four hundred feet. The well was first recorded in 1717, but in all probability it was dug for Timothy fifty years earlier. The other house in the group, end on to the road at the top of Tinkers Lane, was built some years earlier, perhaps before the Civil War. It was the security for a marriage settlement by Edward Andrews, clothworker, of Alton in 1655. Demolished and rebuilt last century, it has been divided in recent years.

However the site with the longest history in Wivelrod, but not part of the Knight estate, is Reedcroft. It can be traced back to the end of the 15th century as a farm called Balams carved out of the common at Hacketts Hill when the Meltons were lords of the manor. It consisted of a messuage with fourteen and a half acres in Vellet

Field, six and a half acres in the South Field of Bentworth and eleven acres in the South Field of Wivelrod, half an acre of woodland at the higher part of Highgrove, Nuttescroft of five acres, Ryecroft of two acres, one acre of meadow, and one croft called Rede of three acres. A new copyhold was granted in 1521.

Lastly there is a cottage, drawn rather incongruously on the map, upside down in the road, another cottage built on the lord's waste. It was then the home of Rose Eames, a widow, and later of James Bramley. In 1837 Roger Fisher, lord of the manor, claimed nine such cottages as copyhold of the manor at a rent of sixpence each, a claim to which the Vestry meeting was ready to agree three years later, but not William Bramley at Maple Cottage, Wivelrod. He refused Fisher's offer of a life interest, and today his descendants are still happily in possession of the property.

News of Randall's surveying in Wivelrod evidently reached the Isle of Wight. In July 1743 a manor court, the first for thirty nine years was held at Hall Farm in the presence of Robert Urry, the surviving son of Thomas. There had been many changes in the long interval, but for the most part the new tenants answered the summons. Of particular interest for this study was the record of eleven cottages which had been built on the waste, five of them at Holt Lane End, the others at Tickley near Burkham, beside Down Well at Well Lane, and the one at Wivelrod. Most of them were already in multiple occupation, housing nineteen widows and/or families, a condition that lasted in general until the First World War.

Thomas Couthard

So far little has been said about the development of Burkham because, regrettably, the records no longer exist; they were burnt as rubbish when the estate was sold. It appears that in addition to the home farm of the Magewicks, there was another farm which belonged to the Hockley family, and perhaps two smallholdings, as well as labourers cottages.

When George Magewick, the last of his line at Burkham, died in 1736, in his ninetieth year, the estate passed to his son-in-law James Battin of Burley in the New Forest, whose wife Elizabeth had died in the birth of their only son. James Battin, with his young son, made his home at Burkham, and in the same year that George died, was made High Sheriff. Twenty five years later his son James Magewick Battin was appointed a Deputy Lieutenant of the County by the Duke of Bolton, and as he, the younger James, began buying land in the village about the same time, the early 1760s, to add eventually to the Burkham estate, the informal role of the village squire became a natural corollary. His first important acquisition was the old farm at Swains in Drury Lane, of about a hundred acres, which for three or four generations had belonged to a younger branch of the Magewick family. It was followed in 1766 by the purchase of Binstead Hill, now Bentworth Lodge, with about three hundred acres, much of it old downland which George Wither had walked with his sheep a hundred and sixty years earlier. Battin also contemplated buying Corporation Farm which lay between Burkham and Swains. A note in the Basingstoke Town Minutes reads, "Tell Mr. Battin, if he will give three thousand guineas, and the value of the timber, he shall have the estate." However there was the charitable status of the farm to be considered, and Battin was probably advised not to buy.

On January 21st 1775 Gilbert White of Selborne wrote in his diary, "Received two bramblings from Mr. Battin of Burkham, seen but seldom in these parts." James Magewick Battin died in 1777, by which time he was probably the owner of a thousand acres, not far short of a third of the village. There is some divergence of opinion about the surviving part of the old house. It may be early eighteenth century, and therefore built by George Magewick; but there are some features, especially the canted bay window in the gothic gable end, and the style of the parapet, which are reminiscent of the south front of The Vyne at Sherborne St. John, designed by John Chute, which suggests they may have been copied by Battin in the last few years of his life. His will recalls the elegant way of life of a country gentleman of the period with the reference to "all my plate, jewels, books, pictures, prints, china... my coach, chariot and all coach and saddle horses". There was also an interesting provision of £10,000 for a fund to finance mortgages to tenants at three per cent; but it seems unlikely that it was implemented. All the farms in the estate were settled on his son Joseph, who was living at Preston Candover; and for his daughter Mary he left a comfortable dowry of another £10,000. A little more than a year after the death of her father Mary married Thomas Coulthard, nephew of his London solicitor. Sadly she died in childbirth four years later, leaving young Thomas, about twelve months old, and the infant, James Battin Coulthard. Few could have envisaged that thirty years hence they would inherit more than half the land in the village.

It is possible that Thomas Urry, grandson of the first lord of the manor of that name, was not unaware of the changes taking place in the village in these years. His steward held four courts at roughly three year intervals between 1759 and 1769. Then the interest subsided again for another thirty years. Urry, who was a bachelor, died in 1776, a few months before Battin, and his estate, including the manor of Bentworth, and another also inherited from Thomas Turgis, the manor of Effingham in Surrey, passed in trust to his sister, her daughter, and about 1800 to his great nieces who married two brothers living in Lancashire. But Urry had a natural son who bore his name and was living in Bentworth with his wife Jane, sister of Thomas Vickery of East End Farm, and their baby son. Whether he had been promised some property is unclear, but after a lengthy law suit he was given some of the Turgis property in London, and

Swains Farmhouse, demolished 1947.

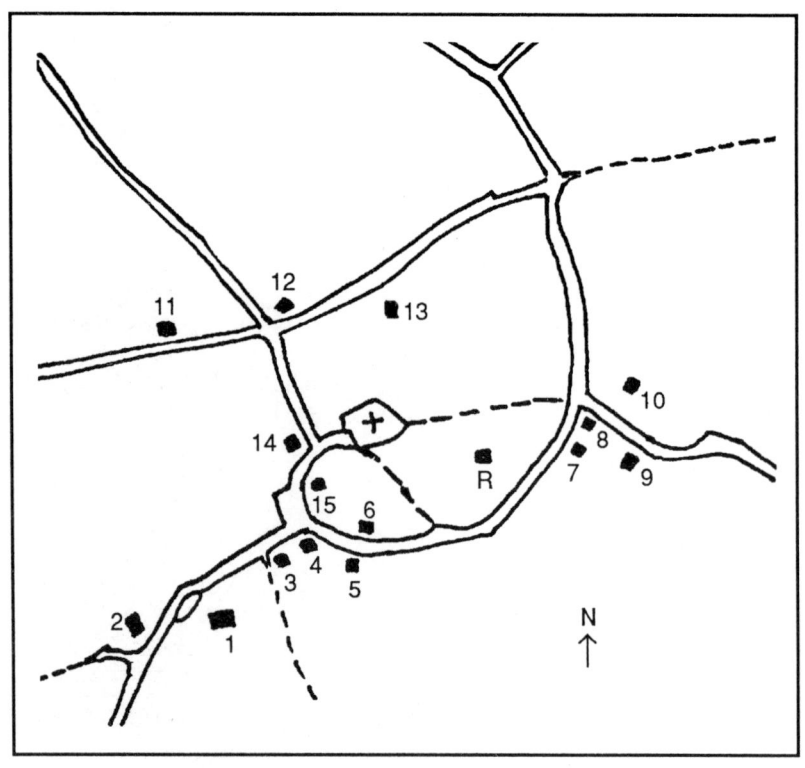

Farmhouses in the centre of the village, with the variations in name which followed changes of ownership.

1. Hall (Place) Farm.
2. Weller's (Place).
3. Blundell's, Blundens.
4. Paices, Henwood's.
5. Fleet's, Ivall's.
6. Westbrook's, Murrell's.
7. Wood's, Ham's, Andrew's, Parsonage Farm.
8. Hewlett's, Gunners.
9. East End Farm.
10. Croucher's, Page's.
11. Page's, Winter's.
12. Eyres, Newman's.
13. Swains, Hailey Dean.
14. King's, Poorhouse.
15. Wither's, Gregory's, Hunt's.

R. The Rectory.

retired to Gosport.

At the time that Coulthard married Mary Battin it is unlikely that he had any thought of buying land or property in Bentworth. He had been born in Cumberland, had made his way to London, and most of his life preferred to live in large rented houses – in Farleigh, Alresford, and from 1800 to 1807 at Chawton House. Jane Austen seems to have kept a respectful distance from him, but liked his wife Frances, "a good hearted, friendly woman". Only at the end of his life did he live at Burkham. The source of his income, apart from Mary's dowry and another from Frances, is a mystery. The family had various connections with the sea as shipbuilders and mariners, and there is a tradition that as a young man he was a privateer who had the luck to share in some rich French or American prize.

However as time passed Coulthard's interest in Burkham was quickened by the prospect of his elder sons, Mary's boys, eventually inheriting the Battin estate as Joseph, her brother, was childless. With that as an incentive he began the long process of buying Corporation Farm, commissioning surveys (three have survived) and supervising the progress of the Humble Petition to Parliament. It stressed the low rent which provided an income sufficient to maintain only six boys at Aldworth's school. At last in December 1795 Hoare's Bank was instructed to transfer to the Mayor, Aldermen, and Burgesses of the town of Basingstoke stock to the value of £3,800.

Having successfully masterminded the Basingstoke Private Act, four years later in 1799 he promoted the Medstead and Bentworth Enclosure Act. There were still 122 acres remaining in the Bentworth open fields, mainly in Wivelrod Field, the old South Field, with a few pieces in Ridge Field and in Cogdell Field to the north of Wadgetts Lane. Coulthard's apportionment was 66 acres, and he bore two thirds of the costs. Six other farmers were involved, Thomas Vickery of East End Farm, Thomas Hall of Preston Candover for Fleet's, then farmed by James Ivall – hence the modern name for the farmhouse, John Andrews of Ropley for Wood's Farm, in later years Parsonage Farm, Joseph Page of Lasham for Croucher's Farm, now Summerley, William Winter for his farm in Ashley Lane now Hop Bine Cottage, and John Paddick at Holt Lane.

With so much of the village in Coulthard's hands some redistribution and rationalisation of the land of the old farms was possible. Part of the Corporation land was added to a small farm called Cooper's at Ashley, some to Swains, and some to Weller's and King's, two tenancies which had been run together for many years, and were now owned by Coulthard. (The timber framed barn which dominates the yard at Weller's was built by Thomas King in 1767.) The remaining part of Corporation Farm was renamed Poles Close Farm, later Powells, from the name of the meadow where the new farmhouse was built, and let to Thomas Goodchild.

By a most fortunate coincidence the first Board of Agriculture survey was published at this time, 1801. The government alarmed by the discontent in the country caused by rising food prices after a series of bad harvests, and made worse by wartime conditions, asked the local clergy to provide an analysis of the acreages in production in their parishes. The newly instituted rector of Bentworth, Henry Close, was among those who responded. He reported 550 acres of wheat, 150 acres of barley, 360 acres of oats, 100 acres of turnips and 30 acres of peas. About 500 acres were under clover, sainfoin and artificial grasses; and stock was calculated at twelve to fifteen hundred sheep and thirty cows. Forty years later at the time of the tithe award the surveyors recorded that the arable land totalled 2760 acres and permanent pasture 256 acres. Either the figures available to the rector had been incomplete, or in the interval another thousand acres of the old grassland had been taken into the rotational system for improvement.

Coulthard died in 1811, and Joseph Battin a year later. Burkham passed to the young Thomas, and his brother James Battin Coulthard was given Binstead Hill, Swains, Poles Close Farm and Ashley, but charged with legacies to his stepmother, Coulthard's widow Frances, and their children. All the farms were in the hands of tenants, and any immediate need of cash was probably met by the executors' sale of Weller's and King's to John Hankin, whose family had been the tenants of Hall Place Farm for many years.

In 1815, the year of Waterloo and the end of high prices for farmers, James married the daughter of an Alton brewer, and the couple lived for some years in the town at 6 High Street, an attractive

The MAGEWICK, BATTIN, COULTHARD family of Burkham

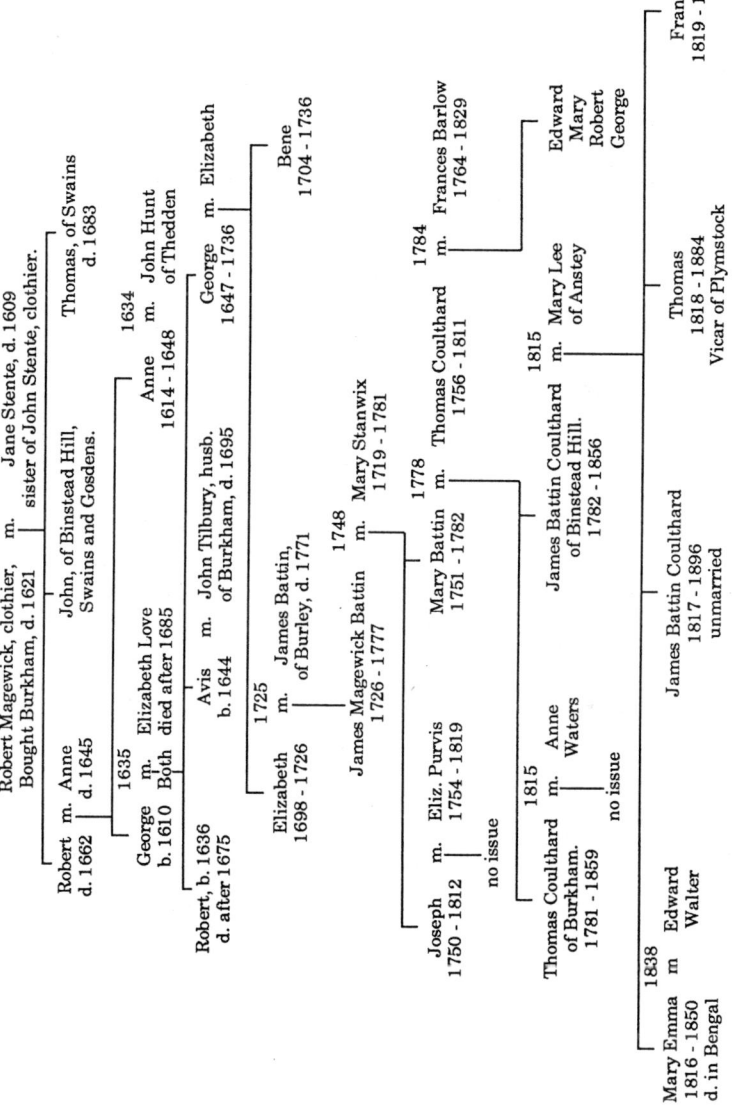

house on Crown Hill which had been his grandmother's marriage settlement. Eventually, about 1824, he came back to the village having built a new house, the present Bentworth Lodge, on the top of the downs. In later years as the agricultural depression continued, it is apparent from the memoranda enrolled by his stepbrother Edward, a barrister, in the manor rolls, that James was not meeting the commitments placed on him by his father's will. He could not; as his solicitors admitted long after his death in retirement at Bath in 1856, they did not seek probate of his will because "there was nothing to prove".

His elder son, another James Battin Coulthard, took over the farm sometime in the 1840s, but the position did not improve. Extreme weather conditions, particularly bad for farmers on clay, led to poor harvests and disease in sheep, but now the shortage of supplies no longer brought about compensatory higher prices, because of the growing volume of imports. It is noticeable that there were frequent changes of tenants at Hall Farm during the same years; even Thomas Parker, a well known Hampshire Down sheep breeder, sold out in 1862 after a particularly bad run of seasons. The beginning of the end came for James B. Coulthard in 1865 when the family started proceedings in the Chancery Court. Poles Close Farm was sold in 1870 and Binstead Hill, Swains and Ashley in 1873. Only Burkham, which had come to him from his uncle Thomas in 1859, was left, and that was put on the market in 1882 when he was declared bankrupt. All that remained was Jerome North's old cottage in Holt Lane which was held in trust for the life of his old servant Jane Laney. In the space of a hundred years the villagers had witnessed the remarkable rise and fall of the Coulthard family as their largest landowners.

The Beginning of the Modern Village

In 1725 the rector Edward Acton, in answer to a Diocesan Visitation enquiry, counted his parishioners, appropriately one might say, as a shepherd did his flock. He estimated he had the care of fifteen or sixteen score souls, between 300 and 320 inhabitants. The first official census in 1801 recorded a population of 425, and in the following decades the figure rose quickly to a peak of 647 in 1861. Since then it has only twice been over the six hundred mark, in 1891 at 604, and in 1951 at 614. By 1981 the figure had fallen to 561.

But where were all these people living? There are no Victorian terraces, and the small scatter of paired, or nowadays semi-detached, cottages built by three land owners and the rector, at dates varying from the early to the late nineteenth century, does not suggest a response to a housing crisis. Families tended to be larger then, and many took in lodgers; houses originally built for one family were divided to accommodate two or even three. By the 1820s the old farmhouses, Gunner's and Ivall's, were farm workers cottages; and King's farmhouse was the parish poorhouse for more than forty years before being sold in 1844 to a "proprietor of houses", a landlord, to convert into six tenements. Swains having been occupied by a tenant farmer, James Andrews, with a family of eleven, plus two carters living in, was divided in the 1850s between two labourers' families, fifteen in all.

What was happening in various areas of the village can be detected by a closer look at the 1851 census returns for Holt Lane End. In addition to the original four seventeenth century houses, two more were built in the eighteenth century on old Tilboroe land which had been sold off for smallholdings. In the last few years both had been bought in by the lord of the manor as estate cottages. There were also the five cottages which had been built on the waste, and by the time of the Tithe Award four of them were in the hands of the Churchwardens and Overseers of the Poor. In 1851 one was divided between three households and accommodated fifteen people; another sheltered sixteen, including a family of nine. Altogether the census of that year listed ninety three people living in the hamlet, divided among twenty households, where now there are twelve.

Overcrowding, and the squalor that often went with it, was but one of the hardships; poverty was another; and there was the ever present threat of the workhouse if some misfortune made them destitute, as so easily happened. Except for Henry Parrack, a painter and glazier, who owned his house, now Holt Green, all the men at Holt Lane End were agricultural labourers, born in Bentworth or within a few miles of the village. Two of them had sons, aged ten and eleven, working with them in the fields; and Parrack described his niece, aged nine, as a "servant of all work". According to the accounts of James Yalden, who farmed at Powells in the 1840s and employed some of these men, carters were paid 9s. a week and £3 at Michaelmas after haymaking and harvest. Boys of sixteen were paid 4s. 6d., and women 2s. 9d. for five and a half days weeding, and 1s. 6d. for two days haymaking. The girls went weeding, turnip pulling, and cow keeping. For all of them the hours were long, for men fourteen hours a day, and the work hard; the only respite came in bad weather when they could not work, and received no pay.

Perhaps in such circumstances it is not surprising that some found the courage to leave their families and familiar surroundings for ever to make a fresh start on the other side of the world. In 1848 four young men and the sister of one of them left the village for Adelaide, South Australia, on an assisted emigration scheme supported by Abraham Crowley. They were followed in time by others, including an orphaned younger brother. Crowley, a Quaker and local benefactor, had bought Baverstock's Brewery in Alton in 1821, and in the space of a few years built up the London trade in Alton Ales. The knock-on effect was that the growth in the brewing industry in the town provided work for men from the villages, and some of them, in particular the carters whose skill lay in their experience of working with heavy horses, were offered jobs in the brewery's London yard as draymen.

Most of the labourers and their families at this time were illiterate, but that too was about to change. The new rector Henry Staverton Mathews, who came to the village in 1847, had the immediate intention of starting a school, and it was built the following year on the site of a fir plantation belonging to the glebe. It consisted of only one schoolroom, with an entrance in the centre of the front wall, and a teacher's cottage next to it under the same roof. Three years later 102 children were described in the census as scholars, out of a possible 127 of school age, generally between six and thirteen. A full attendance would have been a serious embarrassment, but there was no chance of that. Some boys as young as nine, ten and eleven, were described as agricultural labourers. Nevertheless it seems as though most parents tried to give the children at least three years schooling, because younger brothers, and often older sisters were at school. One girl of fifteen staying in the school cottage was listed as a teacher while another of the same age from Holt Lane End was still a scholar. Perhaps she was a monitor waiting to become a trainee teacher. At last the children had a possible alternative to following their parents into the fields and domestic service for the rest of their lives.

Reading through the census schedules, and in effect following in the footsteps of John Hooker, the enumerator, the village emerges by 1851 as a more familiar place. Starting at the house next to his own, the Rectory (now Mulberry House), Hooker tramped along the lanes and across the fields, stopping at each house in turn. Some have since been demolished, some rebuilt, and many spaces have been filled as the number of houses increased. Yet the village plan is much the same. The difference is in the social and economic character of the community. Then the villagers, except for three with an investment income, were dependent on the prosperity of the farms for their wellbeing and livelihood, whether the head of the household was a farmer or a labourer, a tradesman or a pauper on outrelief. Fortunately the village, despite the poverty, was large enough to support the small shops and common skills which made it self-sufficient in its day-to-day requirements. There was a baker and two grocers, three boot and shoe makers (evidence of the toll of living in a clay with flints area), a tailor, two blacksmiths and two wheelwrights, a carpenter, builder, and two painters and glaziers. At the time Hooker was one of the shoemakers, but later he took on an apprentice and developed the business as a baker and grocer, general store and post office. The butcher, Henry Windibank, was also a man of many parts, cordwainer, in other words another shoemaker, victualler, and the tenant of the Sun Inn at East End.

The Sun put up its sign about 1838, but the house had been a copyhold of the manor for a hundred years. The first clue to its use as a pub is an entry in the church register in 1828 which recorded the baptism of a son of William Withers, innkeeper. A court entry of a transfer of ownership ten years later to Henry Gardener of Holybourne, brewer, contains the note "now called the Sun Inn".

The Star was built by Giles Willis, bricklayer, on "part of Pound Meadow, adjoining the site of a blacksmith's shop", for his wife Sophia in 1841. Giles died in 1869, but Sophia carried on until she died in 1885, when the house was bought by Crowley and Co. The Moon, or Half Moon, demolished some years ago, was part of a small farm in Drury Lane opposite Swains. It belonged to William Brown, and was licensed by 1851. His granddaughter's memory of him was the sight of him hurrying off to his fields, his smock billowing in the wind like a balloon. She thought he was probably the last man in the village to wear a smock.

To complete this picture of the village it is necessary to return to the year 1832 when the last links with the descendants of Thomas Urry, lord of the manor, were severed. The Manor of Bentworth and Hall Place Farm were sold at auction in the celebrated surroundings of Garroway's Coffee House in London to Roger Staples Norman Fisher. The sale catalogue shows that much of the land belonging to the farm was still in detached parcels, unlike the Coulthard farms. There was even one last one acre strip, relic of the old South Field, despite the enclosure act of thirty years earlier. It was a hundred and sixty years since the lord of the manor had lived at the farm, and it is doubtful whether much more than essential repairs had been done to the old house, except that the medieval open hall, the court room, had been ceiled over to make a large farmhouse kitchen. The room above, under the rafters, was probably the "servants room" listed in the catalogue, and perhaps partly partitioned as one of the several store rooms not otherwise located.

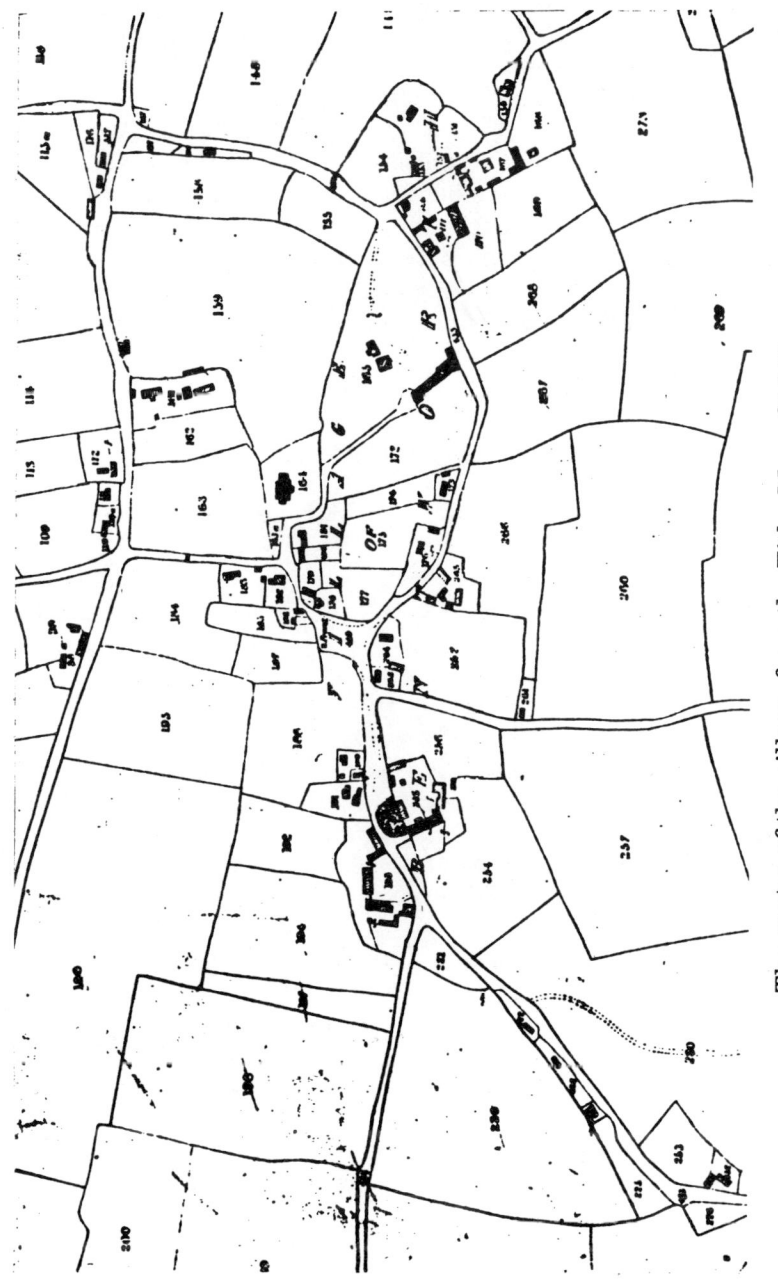

The centre of the village, from the Tithe Map of 1840.

The Village Green c.1905.
On the right the thatched farmhouse built by George Wither, senior. In the centre the double pile of King's Framhouse, later the Poorhouse, and at this time diveded in to cottages.

Almost immediately after his arrival in the village Fisher started planning the building of Bentworth Hall on Westcott Down in the park, once part of the Holt. Ten years later the estate was offered for sale again, this time with a "newly erected Elizabethan mansion of unique elevation". It was built of knapped flints with stone quoins and Tudoresque mullion windows. In profile the stone-edged gable ends rising high above the front parapet gave the impression in a drawing in the catalogue that the roof had fallen in! Fortunately with the railways now spreading out from London the village was no longer quite as remote as it had been and viewing was encouraged. Prospective buyers were recommended to travel by the five o'clock train from Nine Elms to Winchfield on the Southampton line. From there a carriage would take them to Alton for the night. In the morning they could hire another to the village, and then return to London from Basingstoke Station. In 1848 when the estate was again for sale the railway was said to be "nearly completed to Alton". In fact the Farnham to Alton link was opened in 1852.

The estate was finally sold towards the end of 1850 to Jeremiah Robert Ives, J.P. who came of a much respected Norfolk family. In 1854 he was appointed High Sheriff of Hampshire. Unfortunately he died at the comparatively early age of fifty three in 1865, but the estate remained with the family until after the First World War. In the 1870s his son Colonel Gordon Maynard Gordon-Ives built Gaston Grange on the site of a small farm in Gaston Wood, and in 1885 bought Weller's Farm to add to Hall Farm. For some years the two were known as Manor Farm, and Weller's farmhouse became Manor Lodge.

Meanwhile Captain Frederick Stephens had bought Binstead Hill Farm. He renamed it Bentworth Lodge, and built a fine new farm with good brick and flint buildings on the site of an old farm at Childer Hill. The trio of large estate owners was completed in 1883 when Arthur F. Jeffreys, M.P. later Deputy Speaker of the House of Commons, became the owner of Burkham.

All three played their part in the affairs of the village, as did three more strong-minded men less happily matched, the rector, the Rev. Dr. W.A. Cazalet, the Congregational leader, William Murrell, and the school master Charles Penson. William Cazalet came to the village in 1887. Apart from the glebe he also owned Parsonage Farm, formerly Wood's Farm, which a predecessor had bought some forty years earlier. Together they totalled about 180 acres, and were farmed for him by Edward T. Parker, son of Thomas, father of Tom, a family of remarkable Hampshire farmers. Murrell came of a line of Dissenters. His father, Thomas, had registered an Independent Meeting House in Bentworth in April 1824, and a Chapel in Butt Meadow, belonging to William Hankin, six months later. But it was not a success, Murrell moved away, and the house became a grocer's shop. In the 1880s William Murrell, a small farmer with land in Medstead and Bentworth, came back to the village, in the first place to Chapel Cottage. He was a staunch supporter of Gladstone, and convinced that tithes were the ruin of the British farmer. In the preface to a collection of poems published in 1888, soon after Cazalet's arrival, he wrote,

> "Will Whistle is a dissenter, was born so, bred so, is likely to continue so; he does not look so much at what dissenters are, he looks more after the principle of the thing: Will Whistle does not like oppression, or priest-craft, or popery, and he finds too much of all these in the Established Church .... In politics Will Whistle is a radical, believing that only radical measures will suit the present condition of the United Kingdom."

Yet he was a kindly man, a supporter of the under-dog, a man to whom the villagers went for help and advice. In 1896 a new Congregational Chapel was built next to Chapel Cottage, and it is said the people in the village went to church on Sunday morning and to chapel in the evening – because they enjoyed the hymn singing.

Charles Penson came to the village in September 1880, and after a few months was almost in despair. "Compulsory attendance is a dead letter here". In November some of the children were still absent, "employed by the farmers though under age". In 1883 ninety seven were enrolled, and the average attendance was in the seventies, in good weather up into the eighties. By 1889, 129 were enrolled, and the daily average was over a hundred. But the improvement was a serious embarrassment. A second classroom had been added in 1871 for the infants, and now a gallery was installed to provide more seating. But he still had to compete with the pressures of the farming year in the face of the labourers' poverty. Stone picking in May, haymaking in June and July. Summer holidays lasted as long as the harvest. Hopping in September and October, "the boys lead the horses, the girls mind the babies while their mothers are in the fields". In October parents were sending the children to pick acorns for the pigs, and in November and December the boys were beating for the shoots. Finally there was the laconic note, "little ones not coming to school for the rest of the winter".

In 1897, to mark Queen Victoria's Diamond Jubilee, the front entrance was closed and a porch built on the side wall, with a door to each class room. It was some improvement, but far from enough. Eventually in 1911 the Inspector declared the school to be overcrowded, and suitable for only eighty eight children, when there were a hundred and eleven enrolled. Some children walked to school in Lasham while alterations were made. However had Penson managed in the earlier days? When he retired in August 1918 after thirty eight years service he deserved every word of his many testimonials.

Select Bibliography

Victoria County History of Hampshire and the Isle of Wight. (1911) Volume IV.

Baigent, F.J. and Millard, J.E. (1889) History of the Ancient Town and Manor of Basingstoke.

Bigg-Wither, Rev. R.F. (1907) Materials for a History of the Wither Family.

Cross, C. (1987) Church and People. 1450 – 1660.

Elton, G.R. (1974) England under the Tudors.

Hill, C. (1964) Society and Puritanism in Pre-Revolutionary England.

Hill, C. (1977) Milton and the English Revolution.

Pelham, R.A. The Agricultural Revolution in Hampshire, with special reference to the Acreage Returns of 1801. (Papers and Proceedings, Hampshire Field Club, 1953).

Sidgwick, F. (ed.) (1902) Poetry of George Wither. 2 vols.

Thirsk, J. (ed.) (1967) Agrarian History of England and Wales, 1500 – 1640.

Thompson, E.P. (1975) Whigs and Hunters: the Origin of the Black Art.

Index

Acton, Edward: 37, 49
Adams, Henry: 38, 39
Agriculture, Board of: 46
Ashley: 1, 7, 11, 13, 46, 48
Aule: 7; Ralph: 7, 11;
  William: 8, 11
Augustine of Burkham: 8
Austen, Jane: 45
Ballchild, William: 30
Basingstoke: 41, 45
Battin, James: 41;
  Joseph: 42, 45;
  Mary: 42, 45;
  James M: 41, 42;
  family tree 47.
Battisford, John: 11, 16
Bentworth (Bynteworthe),
  Margery: 13;
  Matilda: 8, 11;
  Richard: 8, 11;
  William: 8, 11;
  family tree: 14
Bentworth Hall: 55
Bentworth, Little: 8
Bentworth Lodge: 41, 55
Binstead Hill: 41, 46, 48, 55

Bishop's Down: 11
Bradenham: 21
Brokett, John: 31 – 32
Burkham: 5, 7, 8, 12, 21, 24, 41, 55
Cachefreynsh, John: 12
Cazalet, Rev. Dr. W.A: 55, 56
Chapel, Congregational: 56;
  Hall Farm: 8
Childer Hill: 55
Church: 5 – 6, 20 – 21, 23
Civil War: 32 – 33
Common fields: 7, 16, 24, 45
Commons: 12, 16 – 17, 28 – 29
Compton, Robert: 31
Cooper's Farm, Ashley: 46
Corporation Farm: 35 – 36, 41, 45 – 46
Coulthard, James B: 46 – 48;
  Thomas: 41 – 46;
  family tree: 47
Cromwell, Thomas: 19 – 20
Croucher's Farm: 44 – 45
Devenysh, Nicholas: 11 – 12
East End: 16, 24, 34, 45, 52

Fair Virtue: 28
Fellingdean: 17, 28, 29
Fisher, Roger S.H: 40, 55
Fleet's Farm: 45
Gardiner, Stephen Bp: 19 – 20
Gaston Grange: 55
Goodchild, Thomas: 46
Gunner, Lewis: 36 – 37
Gunner's Farm: 16, 49
Haileydean: 17, 29
Hall (Place) Farm: 7 – 8, 9, 15, 16, 19, 23, 24, 35, 52
Hall, Thomas: 45
Hearth Tax: 33
Henwood, John: 36
Holdip, Nicholas: 23, 30
Holt: 16, 28, 55
Holt Croft: 11, 15, 30
Holt Lane: 16, 31, 45
Holt Lane End: 30, 33, 49
Hood, Timothy: 32
Hooker, John: 51 – 52
Hospitallers: 15, 30
Hunt, Robert: 23, 24, 29, 35, 39; William: 30, 34
Inventories: 25, 30, 33 – 34
Ivalls: 36
Ivall's Farm: 45, 49
Ives, Jeremiah: 55; Gordon M.G: 55

Jeffreys, Arthur F. M.P: 55
Kettlewell, John: 39; Timothy: 39
King's Farm: 46, 49
Knight, Edward Austen: 37; John: 37; Thomas: 37
Magewick, George: 41; Robert: 24; family tree: 47
Makyn, Nicholas: 19, 21
Manor of Bentworth: 5, 8, 19, 20, 35, 42, 52
Manor of Bentworth Hall: 11, 24, 35
Manor Farm: 55; Manor Lodge: 55
Mathews, Rev. H.S: 51
Melton, John: 16, 19; William, Archbp: 8; William: 15
Molyns, James: 13; Juliana: 13; Margery: 13; family tree: 14
Moon, the: 52
Murrell, Thomas: 56; William: 55 – 56
Nevill, Edward: 29, 35, 36
New Copse (Coppice): 31
North, Jerome: 31, 48
Paddick, John: 45
Page, Joseph: 45

Palmes, Francis: 20;
  Guy: 19, 29;
  John: 19 – 21;
  Thomas: 20, 30, 36
Parker, Edward: 56;
  Thomas: 48, 56;
  Tom: 56
Parrack, Henry: 50
Parsonage Farm: 45, 56
Penson, Charles: 56
Poles Close: 46
Poor House: 49
Population: 21, 23, 33, 49
Powell, John: 30
Powells Farm: 36, 46
Pykes: 15, 25
Reedcroft: 39 – 40
Rentals: 11, 13
Rother Hatch: 1, 12
Rouen: 2, 5, 8
School: 51, 56 – 57
Slade: 11, 13
Spencer, John: 39
Spenser, Edmund: 25, 26
Star Inn: 52
Starkey, Ralph: 25 – 26
Stephens, Capt. F: 55;
  Thomas: 20
Subsidy: 1327, 8; 1524, 24, 33
Sun Inn: 52
Swains (Swaynes) Farm: 15, 41, 46, 47, 48, 49; illus. 43

Terry, John: 35;
  Thomas: 35
Turgis, Thomas: 35, 42
Urry, Robert: 38, 40;
  Thomas: 35, 42, 52
Waste, houses on: 31, 33, 40
Well: 1, 10, 28, 40
Weller, William: 15
Weller's Farm: 15, 46, 55
Whistle, Will: 56
White, Gilbert: 42
Willhall: 1, 13
Willway, John: 21, 24
Windsor, Andrew: 16, 18, 19:
  Edward: 21;
  Elizabeth: 15;
  Frederick: 23;
  Henry: 23;
  Miles: 15;
  Richard: 13;
  Thomas: 15, 18;
  family tree: 14
Winter's Farm: 45
Wither, George: 24 – 28;
  James: 24;
  Anthony: 24
Wivelrod: 7, 11, 31, 37 – 40
Wolveridge, Sir James: 35
Wood, John: 37, 39
Wood's Farm: 45
Yalden, James: 50